D0604361

ERIB

SUPERCROSS
RACING

BY JACK DAVID

BELLWETHER MEDIA • MINNEAPOLIS, MN

Are you ready to take it to the extreme?
Torque books thrust you into the action-packed world
of sports, vehicles, and adventure. These books may
include dirt, smoke, fire, and dangerous stunts.
WARNING: Read at your own risk.

This edition first published in 2009 by Bellwether Media.

No part of this publication may be reproduced in whole or in part without written permission of the publisher. For information regarding permission, write to Bellwether Media Inc., Attention: Permissions Department, Post Office Box 19349, Minneapolis, MN 55419.

Library of Congress Cataloging-in-Publication Data
David, Jack, 1968–
  Supercross Racing / by Jack David.
    p. cm. — (Torque : action sports)
  Summary: "Photographs of amazing feats accompany engaging information about supercross racing. The combination of high-interest subject matter and light text is intended for readers in grades 3 through 7"—Provided by publisher.
  Includes bibliographical references and index.
  ISBN-13: 978-1-60014-200-0 (hardcover : alk. paper)
  ISBN-10: 1-60014-200-1 (hardcover : alk. paper)
  1. Supercross—Juvenile literature. I. Title.

  GV1060.1455D35 2009
  796.7'56—dc22   2008016611

CONTENTS

WHAT IS
SUPERCROSS RACING?   4

EQUIPMENT   10

SUPERCROSS RACING
IN ACTION   16

GLOSSARY   22

TO LEARN MORE   23

INDEX   24

WHAT IS SUPERCROSS RACING?

A group of loud dirt bikes soars off a jump. Dirt and mud fly up from under their tires as they land. The high-pitched sound of their engines fills the air. The crowd inside the arena roars as the riders race to the finish line. These are the sights and sounds of a supercross race.

Supercross is a type of dirt bike racing. It grew out of the popular sport of motocross. In **motocross**, riders race on large outdoor tracks. Supercross tracks are smaller and tighter than motocross tracks. They're built inside arenas and stadiums.

Supercross racing isn't just about speed. It requires precise turning and jumping. Riders need skill, good equipment, and a little bit of luck to take the checkered flag.

EQUIPMENT

Supercross cycles are built to handle rough ground, sharp turns, and hard landings. The frame of a supercross bike is called the **chassis**. The **suspension system** connects the chassis to the tires. The springs and shock absorbers of the suspension system help supercross bikes handle bumps and jumps. A bike's knobby tires are designed to have a good grip on the track.

There are two kinds of engines used in supercross bikes. **Two-stroke** engines give the most power, but they burn a lot of fuel and pollute the air. **Four-stroke** engines aren't as powerful as two-stroke engines, but they pollute less and get better **fuel mileage**. Most riders today choose four-stroke engines.

fast fact

The earliest dirt bike races were called scrambles. The sport of motocross, and later supercross, grew out of these scrambles.

Riders need safety gear as well. They wear helmets, gloves, and racing suits to protect them if they fall. They wear **body armor** under their suits. The armor is made of tough plastic and foam. It protects a rider if a dirt bike lands on them during a crash.

SUPERCROSS RACING IN ACTION

The world's best supercross riders race in the American Motorcyclist Association (AMA) Supercross Series. They travel to races across the United States and Canada. They earn points for their place in each race. The rider with the most points at the end of the season wins the championship.

Fast Fact

The sport of supercross emerged in the 1970s. Its name was shortened from a 1972 event called the Superbowl of Motocross.

Each AMA race includes twenty riders. They line up at a mechanical starting gate. When the gate drops, the race begins. The riders burst out of the gate and head for the first turn.

The first rider to get to the turn has the **holeshot**. An early lead is a big advantage. Passing on short, tight supercross tracks takes a lot of skill and patience. The riders skid around turns, rattle over bumps, and sail over jumps. The crowd stands and shouts as the riders speed toward the finish line.

GLOSSARY

body armor—a strong, body-fitting piece of plastic and foam that supercross riders wear underneath their clothes to protect them during crashes

chassis—the metal frame of a vehicle

four-stroke—a type of engine in which fuel is burned in a four-stage process; four-stroke engines get good fuel mileage but aren't as powerful as two-stroke engines.

fuel mileage—the average number of miles a vehicle will travel on a gallon of fuel

holeshot—the position of being first to reach the course's first turn; the racer who has the holeshot has an advantage over the other racers.

motocross—a sport similar to supercross in which riders race dirt bikes on longer outdoor courses

suspension system—the springs and shock absorbers that connect the body of a vehicle to its tires

two-stroke—a type of engine in which fuel is burned in a two-stage process; two-stroke engines are powerful but burn a lot of fuel.

TO LEARN MORE

AT THE LIBRARY

David, Jack. *Motocross Cycles*. Minneapolis, Minn.: Bellwether, 2008.

David, Jack. *Motocross Racing*. Minneapolis, Minn.: Bellwether, 2008.

Levy, Janey. *Supercross*. New York: PowerKids Press, 2007.

ON THE WEB

Learning more about supercross racing is as easy as 1, 2, 3.

1. Go to www.factsurfer.com
2. Enter "supercross racing" into search box.
3. Click the "Surf" button and you will see a list of related web sites.

With factsurfer.com, finding more information is just a click away.

INDEX

1970s, 16
American Motorcyclist
  Association (AMA)
  Supercross Series, 16, 18
arenas, 4, 7
body armor, 14
Canada, 16
chassis, 10
checkered flag, 8
engines, 4, 12
finish line, 4, 20
four-stroke engine, 12
fuel mileage, 12
holeshot, 20
motocross, 7, 13
safety equipment, 14
scrambles, 13
stadiums, 7
starting gate, 18
Superbowl of Motocross, 16

suspension system, 10
tires, 4, 10
tracks, 7, 10, 20
two-stroke engine, 12
United States, 16

The images in this book are reproduced through the courtesy of: Rober Cianflone / Getty Images, front cover, pp. 6, 9; Jeff Huffman Photography, pp. 4, 8, 10, 12, 13 (top & bottom), 15, 17 (top & bottom), 18, 19 (top & bottom), 20; AFP / Getty Images, p. 5; TavlikosPhoto Motorsports / Alamy, p. 7; Jeff Kardas / Getty Images, p. 11; Steve Bruhn / Getty Images, p. 21.